W9-AHZ-776

Br,

TO: ~~Amy~~

Love
FROM: ~~Sheila~~
Benecia.

You are on your way!
Keep daring to be! ♡
♡B.

Library of Congress Catalog Card Number: 97-67185

ISBN: 0-679-88284-7

LIFE FAVORS™ is a trademark of Random House, Inc.

Printed in the United States of America 10 9 8 7 6 5 4 3 2 1

Things You Can Be

WHEN YOU BELIEVE IN YOURSELF

by Benecia Aronwald
illustrated by Jill Weber

LIFE FAVORS™
Random House 🏠 New York

You can be anything
you want to be

So don't wait
one more minute

Now's the time
to begin it

Be the someone
you always dreamed
you could be

Someone who runs
a four-minute mile

FINISH

Someone who aspires
to do good deeds

Like helping people
with special needs

Someone who travels

and explores new lands

Someone whose talent flows

from his or her hands

Choose what you want
to do and be

Everyone
needs a
purpose

you see

So ask your heart
and search your soul

Make up your mind
and find
a goal

Courage

Strength
Confidence
and
a very
strong will

You may meet
with obstacles
along the way

Don't be
discouraged
or let your
dream go astray

It's not about
good fortune

$$Lott

A

or luck
or chance

A

J

It's about believing in yourself

beyond your circumstance

So no matter
who you are
Or where you've been
thus far

Follow your dream
and dare to be

Reap What You Sow